SO-ENU-908

Reading STREET
Grade 1

Scott Foresman
Big Book of Poems

PEARSON
Scott Foresman

Editorial Offices: Glenview, Illinois • Parsippany, New Jersey • New York, New York
Sales Offices: Boston, Massachusetts • Duluth, Georgia • Glenview, Illinois • Coppell, Texas
Sacramento, California • Mesa, Arizona

ISBN: 0-328-16889-0 Copyright © Pearson Education, Inc. All Rights Reserved. Printed in the United States of America. This publication is protected by Copyright, and permission should be obtained from the publisher prior to any prohibited reproduction, storage in a retrieval system, or transmission in any form by any means, electronic, mechanical, photocopying, recording, or likewise. For information regarding permission(s), write to: Permissions Department, Scott Foresman, 1900 East Lake Avenue, Glenview, Illinois 60025.

4 5 6 7 8 9 10 V088 12 11 10 09 08

Table of Contents

1. After School
2. Visiting the Vet
3. The Barnyard
4. Pete at the Zoo
5. The Little Turtle
6. Giraffes
7. Family Recipe
8. When the Librarian Reads to Us
9. The Window Cleaner
10. Long Gone
11. Papago Poem *and* Haiku
12. The Bee
13. Growing Up
14. Learning to Ice-Skate
15. A New Friend
16. Isn't It Amazing?
17. The Secret
18. Aliona's Street
19. Surprises
20. City Music
21. My Travel Tree
22. Fourth of July Night
23. Secret Door
24. Next-Door People
25. Dickery Dean
26. Something to Think About *and* Air Station
27. Questions
28. The Vacuum Cleaner's Revenge
29. Crazy Boys
30. Kitchen Percussion

Acknowledgments

"After School" from *Feathered Ones and Furry* by Aileen Fisher. Copyright © 1971 Aileen Fisher. Used by permission of Marian Reiner.

"Visiting the Vet" by Tony Johnston. Reprinted by arrangement with the author and Writers House LLC, acting as agent for the author.

"Pete at the Zoo" by Gwendolyn Brooks from *The Bean Eaters*.

"Giraffes" from *Yellow Butter Purple Jelly Red Black Bread* by Mary Ann Hoberman. Reprinted by permission of The Gina Maccoby Literary Agency. Copyright © 1981 by Mary Ann Hoberman.

"Family Recipe" from *Angels Ride Bikes* by Francisco X. Alarcón. Copyright © 1999 by Francisco X. Alarcón. All rights reserved.

"When the Librarian Reads to Us" by Kalli Dakos. Reprinted with the permission of Simon & Schuster Books for Young Readers, an imprint of Simon & Schuster Children's Publishing Division from *Put Your Eyes Up Here and Other School Poems* by Kalli Dakos. Text copyright © 2003 Kalli Dakos.

"The Window Cleaner" by M. Long.

"Long Gone" from *Zoo Doings* by Jack Prelutsky, 1983.

"A Little Yellow Cricket" (Papago Indian) from *Singing for Power: The Song Magic of the Papago Indians of Southern Arizona* by Ruth Murray Underhill. Copyright © Ruth Murray Underhill, 1938, 1966. Used by permission of The Regents of the University of California.

Gaki: Haiku: "Little Frog," from *Birds, Frogs, and Moonlight*, translated by Sylvia Cassedy and Kunihiro Suetake. Copyright 1967 by Doubleday & Co. By permission of Ellen Cassedy.

"The Bee" from *Is Somewhere Always Far Away?* by Leland B. Jacobs.

"Growing Up" from *The Little Hill Poems & Pictures* by Harry Behn. Copyright 1949 Harry Behn. © Renewed 1977 by Alice L. Behn. Used by permission of Marian Reiner.

"Learning to Ice-Skate" by Laura Numeroff. Reprinted with the permission of Simon & Schuster Books for Young Readers, an imprint of Simon & Schuster Children's Publishing Division from *Sometimes I Wonder if Poodles Like Noodles* by Laura Numeroff. Text copyright © 1999 Laura Numeroff.

"A New Friend" by Marjorie Allen Anderson.

"Isn't It Amazing?" from *Peculiar Rhymes and Lunatic Lines* by Max Fatchen. First published in the UK by Orchard Books in 1995, a division of The Watts Publishing Group Limited, 96 Leonard Street, London EC2A 4XD.

"Aliona's Street" by Emily George.

"Surprises" by Jean Conder Soule. Permission granted by the author.

"City Music" by Tony Mitton, reprinted by permission of Murray Pollinger Literary Agent, David Higham Associates.

"My Travel Tree" by Bobbi Katz.

"Fourth of July Night" from *Hop, Skip and Jump!* by Dorothy Aldis, copyright 1934, renewed © 1961 by Dorothy Aldis. Used by permission of G. P. Putnam's Sons, A Division of Penguin Young Readers Group, A Member of Penguin Group (USA) Inc., 345 Hudson Street, New York, NY 10014. All rights reserved.

"Secret Door" by Myra Cohn Livingston. Reprinted with the permission of Margaret K. McElderry Books, an imprint of Simon & Schuster Children's Publishing Division from *Worlds I Know and Other Poems* by Myra Cohn Livingston. Text copyright © 1985 Myra Cohn Livingston.

"Dickery Dean" by Dennis Lee.

"Something to Think About" by Carolyn Forsyth. From *Jack and Jill*, copyright © 1952 by Curtis Publishing. Used by permission of Children's Better Health Institute, Benjamin Franklin Literary & Medical Society, Inc., Indianapolis, Indiana.

"Air Station" by Emily M. Hilsabeck.

"Questions" by Miriam Clark Potter. Children's Better Health Institute.

"The Vacuum Cleaner's Revenge" by Patricia Hubbell. Copyright © 2001 by Patricia Hubbell. Used by permission of Marian Reiner for the author.

"Crazy Boys" by Beverly McLoughland originally appeared in *Hand in Hand-An American History Through Poetry*, edited by Lee Bennett Hopkins, Simon & Schuster, 1994. Reprinted by permission of the author who controls all rights.

"Kitchen Percussion" by Lynne Berry. *Ladybug*, Sep 2004, Vol. 15, Number 1. Copyright 2004 by Lynne Berry.

After School

My puppy needs a brushing,
though he doesn't know what for,

And then he needs an outing,
and a tussle on the floor,

And then he needs his supper,
and a going-out once more,

And every day I wonder
what I used to do *before*.

by Aileen Fisher

Visiting the Vet

My dog is trembling
in the car.
She feels where we are going.
My dog is huddled
by the door,
worn-out with all that knowing.
So I whisper in her ear,
"I am here, girl. I am here."

by Tony Johnston

The Barnyard

When the Farmer's day is done,
In the barnyard, ev'ry one,
Beast and bird politely say,
"Thank you for my food today."

The cow says, "Moo!"
The pigeon, "Coo!"
The sheep says, "Baa!"
The lamb says, "Maa!"
The hen, "Cluck, Cluck!"
"Quack!" says the duck;
The dog, "Bow Wow!"
The cat, "Meow!" . . . .

When the barn is locked up tight
Then the Farmer says, "Good-night!"
Thanks his animals ev'ry one,
For the work that has been done.

           by Maud Burnham

Pete at the Zoo

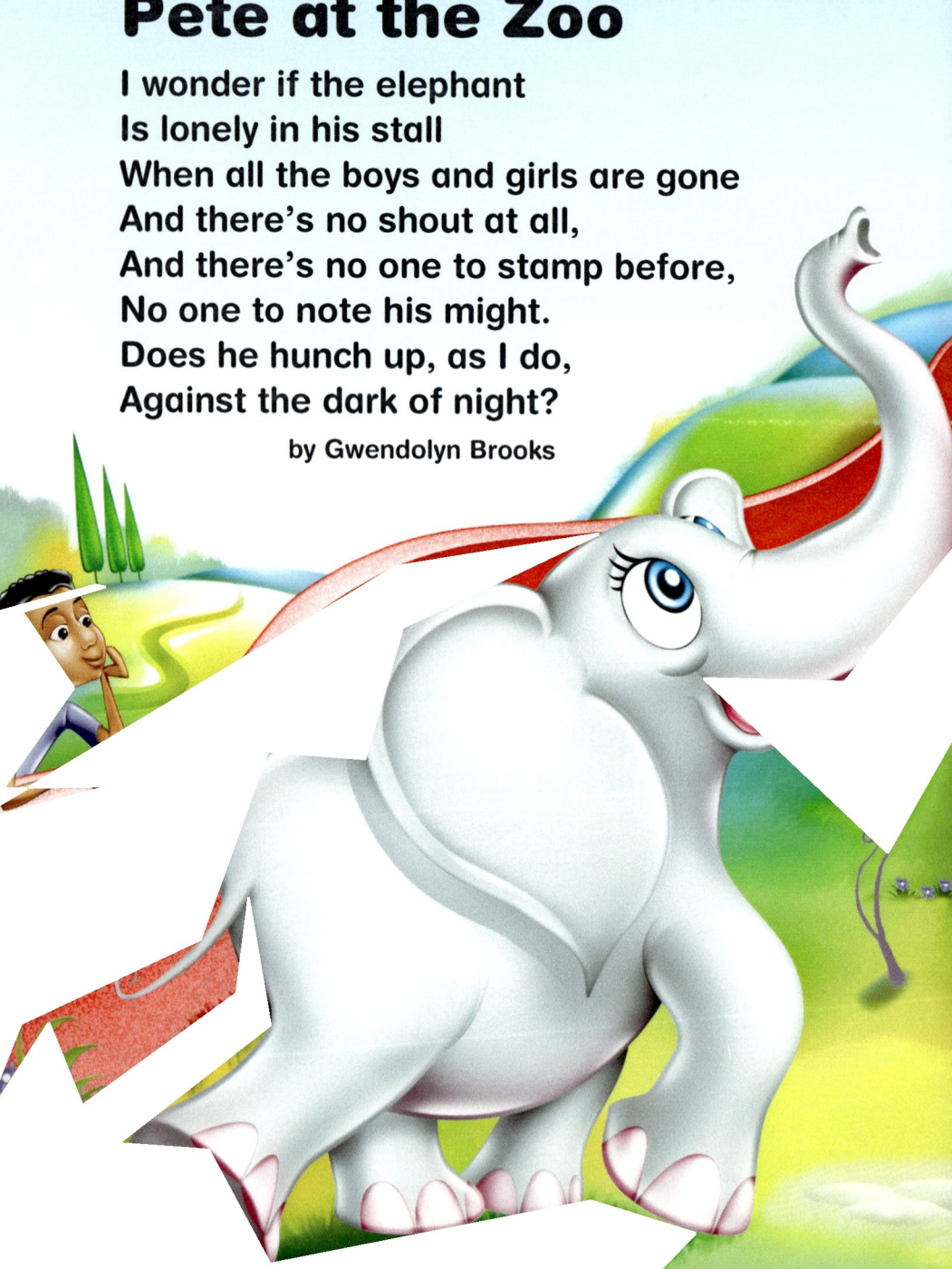

I wonder if the elephant
Is lonely in his stall
When all the boys and girls are gone
And there's no shout at all,
And there's no one to stamp before,
No one to note his might.
Does he hunch up, as I do,
Against the dark of night?

by Gwendolyn Brooks

The Little Turtle

There was a little turtle.
He lived in a box.
He swam in a puddle.
He climbed on the rocks.

He snapped at a mosquito.
He snapped at a flea.
He snapped at a minnow.
And he snapped at me.

He caught the mosquito.
He caught the flea.
He caught the minnow.
But he didn't catch me.

by Vachel Lindsay

Giraffes

I like them.
Ask me why.
    Because they hold their heads so high.
    Because their necks stretch to the sky.
    Because they're quiet, calm, and shy.
    Because they run so fast they fly.
    Because their eyes are velvet brown.
    Because their coats are spotted tan.
    Because they eat the tops of trees.
    Because their legs have knobby knees.
    Because
    Because
    Because. That's why
I like giraffes.

    by Mary Ann Hoberman

Family Recipe

following
an old family
recipe

we all
do our part
in cooking *mole*

I roast
and peel
chili peppers

my sister
grinds walnuts
and chocolate

my father
cuts the turkey
into pieces

my mother
stirs the pot
with a big spoon

adding
a little bit
of this and that

when we all
sit down to eat
my mother tells us:

"this family
is a dream
come true"

by Francisco X. Alarcón

When the Librarian Reads to Us

Goose bump good,
Goose bump good.
The stories she reads
Are goose bump good.

All over my arms,
The goose bumps grow,
For just a moment,
And then they go.

Goose bump good,
Goose bump good,
The stories she reads
Are goose bump good.

by Kalli Dakos

The Window Cleaner

When I grow up I want to be
A window cleaning man
And make the windows in our street
As shiny as I can.
I'll put my ladder by the wall
And up the steps I'll go
But when I'm up there with my pail
I hope the wind won't blow.

by M. Long

Long Gone

Don't waste your time in looking for
the long-extinct tyrannosaur,
because this ancient dinosaur
just can't be found here anymore.

This also goes for stegosaurus,
allosaurus, brontosaurus
and any other saur or saurus.
They all lived here long before us.

by Jack Prelutsky

A little yellow cricket
At the roots of the corn
Is hopping about and singing.
    Papago Indian

Haiku

Little frog among
rain-shaken leaves, are you, too,
splashed with fresh, green paint?
    by Gaki

The Bee

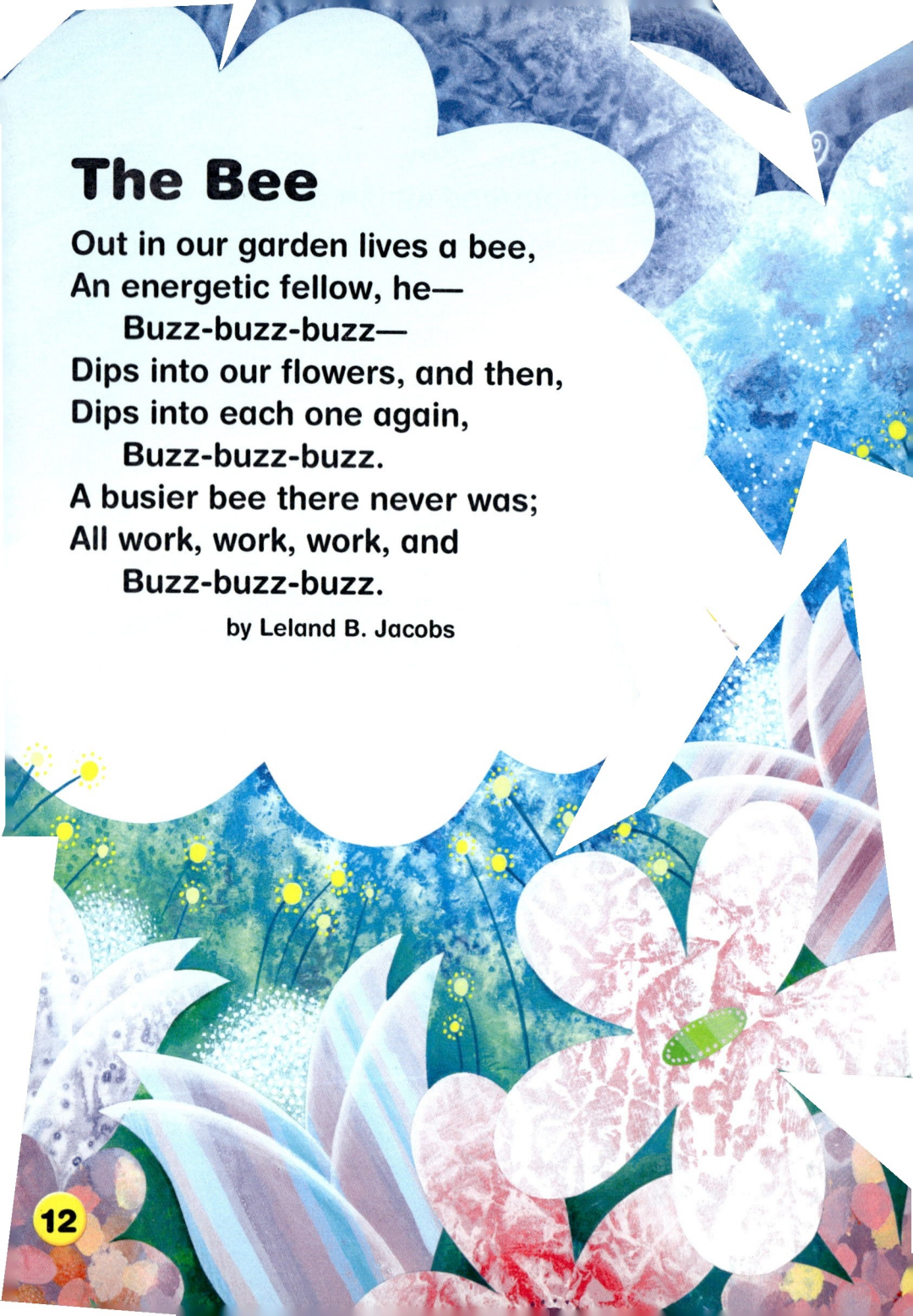

Out in our garden lives a bee,
An energetic fellow, he—
   Buzz-buzz-buzz—
Dips into our flowers, and then,
Dips into each one again,
   Buzz-buzz-buzz.
A busier bee there never was;
All work, work, work, and
   Buzz-buzz-buzz.

by Leland B. Jacobs

Growing Up

When I was seven
We went for a picnic
Up to a magic
Foresty place.
I knew there were tigers
Behind every boulder,
Though I didn't meet one
Face to face.

When I was older
We went for a picnic
Up to the very same
Place as before,
And all of the trees
And the rocks were so little
They couldn't hide tigers
Or *me* anymore.

          by Harry Behn

Learning to Ice-Skate

I'm learning how to ice-skate,
But I'm always falling down.
I guess it's lucky that I'm short,
So I'm closer to the ground.

I'd like to spin around and round,
And do a figure eight.
But I'll have to start with staying up—
Figure eights can wait.

        by Laura Numeroff

A New Friend

They've taken in the furniture;
I watched them carefully.
I wondered, "Will there be a child
Just right to play with me?"

So I peeked through the garden fence
(I couldn't wait to see.)
I found the little boy next door
Was peeking back at me.

by Marjorie Allen Anderson

Isn't It Amazing?

Now isn't it amazing
That seeds grow into flowers,
That grubs become bright butterflies
And rainbows come from showers,
That busy bees make honey gold
And never spend time lazing,
That eggs turn into singing birds,
Now isn't that amazing?

by Max Fatchen

The Secret

We have a secret, just we three,
The robin, and I, and the sweet cherry-tree;
The bird told the tree, and the tree told me,
And nobody knows it but just us three.

But of course the robin knows it best,
Because he built the—I shan't tell the rest;
And laid the four little—something in it—
I'm afraid I shall tell it every minute.

But if the tree and the robin don't peep,
I'll try my best the secret to keep;
Though I know when the little birds fly about
Then the whole secret will be out.

Anonymous

Aliona's Street

My street has a garden
neat and small
that tells me,
"It's summer."
"It's spring."
"It's fall."
But all winter long
it does not make a peep.
Please pass it on tiptoes.
The plants are asleep.

      by Emily George

Surprises

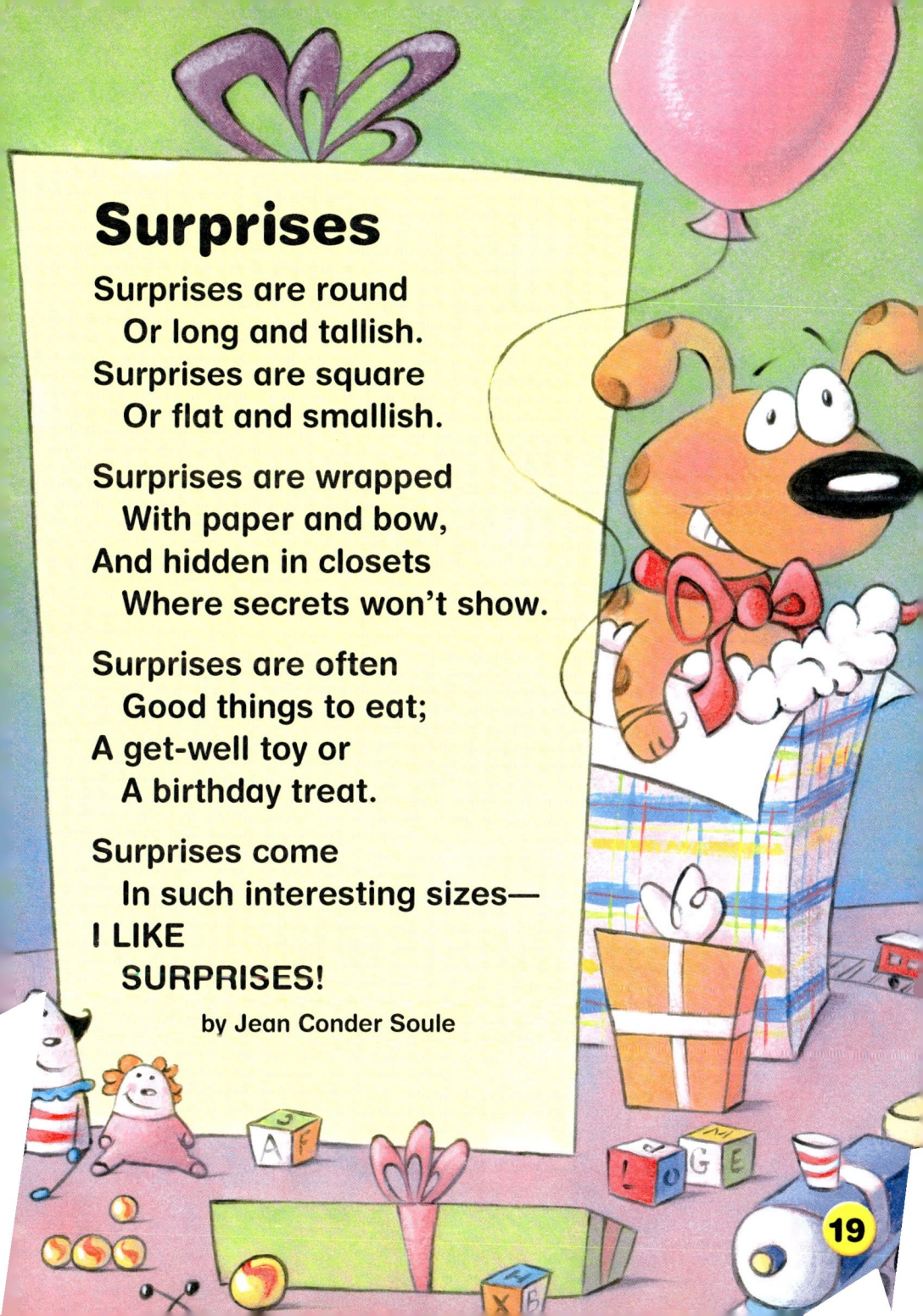

Surprises are round
   Or long and tallish.
Surprises are square
   Or flat and smallish.

Surprises are wrapped
   With paper and bow,
And hidden in closets
   Where secrets won't show.

Surprises are often
   Good things to eat;
A get-well toy or
   A birthday treat.

Surprises come
   In such interesting sizes—
I LIKE
   SURPRISES!

      by Jean Conder Soule

City Music

Snap your fingers.
Tap your feet.
Step out a rhythm
down the street.

Rap on a litter bin.
Stamp on the ground.
City music
is all around.

***Beep** says the motor-car.*
***Ding** says bike.*
City music
is what we like.

　　　　by Tony Mitton

My Travel Tree

There are oh-so-many
kinds of trees—
apple, pear, pine—
but there is just one special tree
I feel is somehow mine.
Its branches form
such cozy nooks
for dreaming dreams
and reading books.
I sail to almost anywhere,
perched among the leaves up there.
If naming things were up to me,
I'd call this one my travel tree.

by Bobbi Katz

Fourth of July Night

Pin wheels whirling round
Spit sparks upon the ground,
And rockets shoot up high
And blossom in the sky—
Blue and yellow, green and red
Flowers falling on my head,
And I don't ever have to go
To bed, to bed, to bed!

        by Dorothy Aldis

Secret Door

The upstairs room
has a secret door.
Dad says someone
used it for
some papers many years ago,
and if I want to, I can go
and bring a treasured thing
to hide and lock it up
all dark inside

and it can be
a place for me
to open
with
its
tiny
key.

by Myra Cohn Livingston

Next-Door People

The next-door people have a bird!
The yellowest you ever heard!
It hops and chirps and sings—and sings!
Aren't next-door people pleasant things!

by Mary Carolyn Davies

Dickery Dean

"What's the matter
 With Dickery Dean?
He jumped right into
 The washing machine!"

"Nothing's the matter
 With Dickery Dean—
He dove in dirty.
 And he jumped out clean!"

by Dennis Lee

Something to Think About

When airplanes get as thick as cars,
And people ride from Earth to Mars,
Will traffic lights be made of stars?
        by Carolyn Forsyth

Air Station

My rocket ship will travel fast,
And it will travel far.
I'll cruise in it to planets
And to the farthest star.

Then, when I've traveled all about,
A station in the air
Will give my ship a checkup,
And I'll start home from there.
        by Emily M. Hilsabeck

Questions

A squirrel running across the park
Carried his tail like a question mark.

He carried his tail that way because
He could not remember where something was!

He'd buried a big, delicious nut,
But where, oh where? He had quite forgot.

If he keeps his tail like a question mark,
He'll find the answer (perhaps) by dark.

    by Miriam Clark Potter

The Vacuum Cleaner's Revenge

I munch. I crunch.
I zoom. I roar.

I clatter-clack
Across the floor.

I swallow twigs.
I slurp dead bugs.

I suck the cat hair
From the rugs.

My stomach full
Of dirt and dust

I gulp another
Pizza crust.

A tiresome life—
All work, no play—

I think I'll swallow you today!

by Patricia Hubbell

Crazy Boys

Watching buzzards,
Flying kites
Lazy, crazy boys
The Wrights. They

Tried to fly
Just like a bird
Foolish dreamers
Strange. Absurd. We

Scoffed and scorned
Their dreams of flight
But we were wrong
And they were Wright.

    by Beverly McLoughland

Kitchen Percussion

Rap on a pot.
Tap on a pan.
Shake macaroni in an old tin can.
Beat on the base of a big wood bowl—
Rattle-tap
Rattle-tap
Rock and roll!

    by Lynne Berry